The Restoration Court Poets

by VIVIAN de SOLA PINTO

Published for the British Council
and the National Book League
by Longmans, Green & Co

Two shillings and sixpence net

The court wits and poets of the Restoration have usually been regarded as talented debauchees. Macaulay's reference to their 'outrageous profaneness and licentiousness' is typical of the moralistic condemnation to which they have been subjected. Professor Pinto argues that 'the merry gang', as Marvell called them, were no mere idle profligates, but intellectuals reacting against the formality of the elder Cavaliers and the narrowness of the Puritans.

He examines the writings of four Court poets, all of whom practised two chief kinds of poetry: the love lyric, and the satire. Although they were amateurs they were not *dilettanti*, and they rendered certain valuable services to English poetry. In particular, they preserved the lyrical spirit in an age dominated by the new scientific movement; and they ensured the continuance in English poetry of a tradition of vernacular and colloquial verse which might otherwise have vanished.

V. de S. Pinto is Emeritus Professor of English at the University of Nottingham. His *Restoration Carnival* (1954) is a detailed study of the poets of the period, and he has edited the poems and written the life of Rochester. His most recent publications in other fields include *Crisis in English Poetry 1880-1940* (1951), *The Common Muse* (1957), which he edited with A. E. Rodway, and an edition, with Warren Roberts, of *The Complete Poems of D. H. Lawrence* (1964).

Bibliographical Series

of *Supplements to* 'British Book News'
on *Writers and Their Work*

GENERAL EDITOR
Geoffrey Bullough

JOHN WILMOT 2nd EARL OF ROCHESTER
from the painting attributed to J. HUYSMANS in the National Portrait Gallery

THE RESTORATION COURT POETS

JOHN WILMOT, EARL OF ROCHESTER
CHARLES SACKVILLE, EARL OF DORSET
SIR CHARLES SEDLEY · SIR GEORGE ETHEREGE

by

VIVIAN de SOLA PINTO

PUBLISHED FOR
THE BRITISH COUNCIL
AND THE NATIONAL BOOK LEAGUE
BY LONGMANS, GREEN & CO

LONGMANS, GREEN & CO LTD
48 Grosvenor Street, London W.1

*Associated companies, branches and
representatives throughout the world*

First published 1965
© Vivian de Sola Pinto 1965

*Printed in Great Britain by
F. Mildner & Sons, London, E.C.1*

CONTENTS

¶ JOHN WILMOT, 2nd EARL OF ROCHESTER was the son of a Cavalier general. Born in 1647, he was educated at Wadham College, Oxford, where he took his M.A. in 1660. He then travelled in France and Italy, returning to England in 1664, when he appeared at court and earned a reputation for wit and dissipation. He served at sea in the Dutch war in 1665-6. Charles II enjoyed his company but he was banished from court more than once for his outspoken satires on the king. His health declined in the late sixteen-seventies and in 1679 he made the acquaintance of Gilbert Burnet, afterwards Bishop of Salisbury, with whom he had a series of conversations on religion in the winter of 1679-80. After a dramatic conversion to Christianity, he died on 26 July 1680.

¶ CHARLES SACKVILLE, 6th EARL OF DORSET, born in 1643, became Lord Buckhurst in 1652 when his father inherited the title of Earl of Dorset. After spending a year at Westminster School, he travelled on the Continent, returning to England soon after the Restoration. He collaborated with Sedley and others in a translation of a tragedy of Corneille, which was produced in 1663, and in June of that year took part with Sedley in a wild frolic at the Cock Tavern in Covent Garden. He served at sea against the Dutch in 1665, and in 1677 inherited the earldom of Dorset. In the House of Lords in 1689 he voted in favour of offering the throne to William and Mary and he became Lord Chamberlain to the new monarchs. He was a generous patron to many men of letters. He died in January 1705/6.

¶ SIR CHARLES SEDLEY (or SIDLEY), born in 1639, was the son of a Kentish baronet. He was educated at Wadham College, Oxford and inherited the baronetcy on the death of his brother in 1656. After the Restoration he became a lively member of the 'merry gang' at court. His comedy *The Mulberry Garden* was staged in 1668, his tragedy *Antony and Cleopatra* in 1677 and a second comedy *Bellamira* in 1687. He was M.P. for New Romney and was a frequent and vigorous speaker in the Commons after the Revolution. He died in August 1701.

¶ SIR GEORGE ETHEREGE, born in 1635, probably spent part of his early life in France, where his father died in 1649. He was apprenticed to a London attorney in 1653 and made the acquaintance of Buckhurst (Dorset) through the success of his play *The Comical Revenge* in March 1664. His second comedy *She Wou'd If She Cou'd* was staged in February 1667-8 and in August 1668 he went to Constantinople as secretary to the British ambassador. He was in London in 1671 and his best comedy *The Man of Mode* was produced with great success in 1676. In 1679 he was knighted, and in 1685 he went to Ratisbon (Regensburg) as British envoy to the Diet of the Empire. At the Revolution he relinquished his post at Ratisbon and went to Paris, where he died in May 1692.

THE
RESTORATION COURT POETS

I

INTRODUCTION

THE last group of English courtier poets belonged to a set of lively young people in whose company Charles II spent much of his time after the Restoration. In 1661 the Duke of Ormonde described them to the Chancellor Clarendon as 'confident young men who abhorred all discourse that was serious, and, in the liberty they assumed in drollery and raillery, preserved no reverence towards God or man, but laughed at all sober men, and even at religion itself'. The historian Burnet gives us the names of some of these 'confident young men': 'the three most eminent wits of that time . . . the earls of Dorset and Rochester and Sir Charles Sidley'. A brilliant addition to the group was George Etherege, who became acquainted with Lord Buckhurst (afterwards Earl of Dorset) as a result of the success of his first play, *The Comical Revenge*, in March 1664. These young men together with the slightly older and immensely rich Duke of Buckingham and a number of less distinguished figures formed the circle known as the Court Wits, described by Andrew Marvell as 'the merry gang', who led a gay, dissipated life in the sixteen-sixties and -seventies, the period called by Dryden 'A very Merry Dancing, Drinking, Laughing, Quaffing, and unthinking Time'. Legends clustered round the personalities of the Wits, and they were built up into figures of diabolical wickedness in the age of the new puritanism which followed the Revolution. Macaulay in the second chapter of his *History of England* speaks in horrified tones of 'the open profligacy of the court and Cavaliers' after the Restoration and 'the outrageous profaneness and licentiousness of the Buckinghams and the Sedleys'. Unfortunately criticism of their writings was for long coloured by this moralistic condemnation of their lives. Now that the great flood of

7

English puritanism has subsided it is possible to see the Wits and their writings in a truer perspective.

They were certainly no mere idle profligates. Their diversions included music, the theatre, reading and translating the classics, and literary discussion as well as women and drinking. Both Rochester and Buckhurst fought as volunteers at sea in the Dutch war. Rochester, surprisingly, seems to have been an affectionate, if not a faithful, husband and a good landlord. Dorset (Buckhurst) was a generous and discerning patron of poets and dramatists. Sedley, after a riotous youth, became a useful member of the House of Commons, and Etherege was a successful dramatist and later, by seventeenth-century standards, an efficient diplomat. They were men living between two worlds, on the one hand the old hierarchical universe mirrored in the traditional life of the Court, on the other the new materialistic philosophy and science and the atomized society of free individuals. They can be seen now not, as they have been traditionally pictured, a set of young royalists indulging in wild orgies as a reaction from the austerity of the Rule of the Saints, but as a post-war generation reacting as much against the stiff formality of the old cavaliers as against the narrow religiosity of the puritans. They were intellectuals as well as gay young men about town. Both Rochester and Sedley received part of their education at Wadham College, Oxford, one of the cradles of the new experimental science, and they all read and admired the works of Thomas Hobbes, the first English philosopher to propound a purely materialistic and utilitarian system. Hobbes was to them something very much like what Marx was to the young English poets of the nineteen-thirties, a symbol of liberation from antique inhibitions and out-worn ideas. Sedley, addressing a typical Court Wit, wrote:

> Thou art an Atheist, Quintus, and a Wit,
> Thinkst all was of self-moving Attoms made.

If Hobbes was right and the universe consisted merely of

atoms governed by mathematical laws, it was surely only sensible to enjoy the good things of this world and ignore the croakings of killjoys, whether they were anglican parsons, puritan preachers or old fashioned cavaliers. The age was one of experiment, and the Wits tried the experiment of living in a little pagan paradise of sensual, aesthetic and intellectual pleasure. Behind the experiment there was a vision and a theory. The vision was well described by Charles Lamb as 'the Utopia of gallantry, where pleasure is duty and the manners perfect freedom'. The theory was that which was known in seventeenth-century Europe as 'libertinism',[1] a term which implied a revolt against traditional morality and institutions and a way of life based on the satisfaction of natural passions and appetites. Rochester, who had the most philosophical mind of the group summed up the libertine theory in the following lines:

> Thus, whilst 'gainst false reas'ning I inveigh,
> I own right Reason, which I wou'd obey;
> That Reason, which distinguishes by sense,
> And gives us rules of good and ill from thence:
>
>   *   *   *
>
> Your Reason hinders, mine helps t' enjoy,
> Renewing Appetites, yours wou'd destroy.

The attempt to live in accordance with these principles was bound to fail in the face of the realities of the human condition, but the vision which lay behind it, as well as the contradictions which it involved, provided material for the best comedies of the period as well as for the poetry of the courtiers.

The Wits must not be judged as professional poets. Like their predecessors, the Cavalier poets of the Court of Charles I, they were gentlemen amateurs and their verses, which were mostly 'occasional', were written not for publication

[1] It is well described by Dale Underwood in *Sir George Etherege and the Seventeenth Century Comedy of Manners* (1957), pp. 10-36.

in the modern sense of the word but for circulation in manuscript among their friends. This does not mean that they were mere *dilettanti*, for whom the writing of verse was simply an elegant game. This was, doubtless, true of the minor figures in the Court circle, but, for the leading Wits, poetry was an art and a vital expression of a truly creative culture founded on a knowledge of books and experience of life. They aimed at what they called 'ease' or colloquial naturalness in poetry and were well aware that this could only be achieved by craftsmanship, even though their practice was sometimes marred by gentlemanly carelessness. Their poetry belongs to the courtly-classical or polite tradition, which descends from Ben Jonson through the Cavalier poets of the reign of Charles I. This tradition under-went a change somewhere about the middle of the century, when it began to acquire the character which we call Augustan. The change is apparent in the poetry of Waller and Cowley, two poets of the mid-century whose work was greatly admired by the Wits. Hobbes, who was influential both as a literary critic and a philosopher, had close connec-tions with both these poets, and in their best work they are trying to carry into effect his demand for a new 'perspicuity', worldliness and realism in poetry.[1] They saw themselves as new Augustans renovating English poetry after the English Civil War as Virgil and Horace renovated Latin poetry after the Civil Wars of Rome. This new 'Augustan' move-ment could tend either towards a greater actuality and realism in accordance with the spirit of the new science and the new philosophy, or towards an elegant rococo neo-classicism not without charm but always in danger of becoming pompous and insipid. Both tendencies are apparent in the poetry of the Wits. At its worst it is not very far removed from Etherege's parody of the fashionable love lyric in *The Man of Mode* (1676):

---

[1] See his 'Answer to Davenant' (1650) in *Critical Essays of the Seventeenth Century*, ed. J. E. Spingarn, II, 63.

How Charming Phillis is, how fair!
Ah that she were as willing,
To ease my wounded heart of Care
And make her Eyes less killing.

But in their best poetry they were saved from this kind of thing by their good sense, their wit and their irony. They were helped, too, by their contact with a tradition which is commonly ignored by the literary historians. This was the tradition of the street ballad and popular song, that lusty growth of English vernacular poetry found in innumerable broadsides sold in the streets and taverns and in the popular verse miscellanies such as the *Drolleries* and *Academies of Compliments*, which were best-sellers in the Restoration bookshops.

The two chief kinds of poetry which they practised were the love lyric and the satire or 'libel'. The two kinds often tend to shade into each other in their work and one of its distinguishing marks is the combination of the singing voice of the lyric with the critical and ironic spirit of satire. They were the last English poets to use successfully the pastoral convention as part of the courtly love-game. This convention had lost the imaginative grandeur with which it was invested in the High Renaissance, but it remained a symbol for a non-moral dream-world of delicate charm and grace. At the end of the century it had become absurd when Lady Wishfort in Congreve's *The Way of the World* (1700) proposed to 'retire to deserts and solitudes, and feed harmless sheep by groves and purling streams'. The Wits in their best lyrics avoid this sort of silly escapism by disinfecting the pastoral with what Ezra Pound called 'a dash of bitters'. With them reality, like cheerfulness in the philosophy of Dr. Johnson's friend, kept breaking in. At times, too, their realistic temper enables them to use the convention to express a human situation when it becomes clear that Thirsis or Strephon is a real man feeling a genuine affection for his Celia and Phillis. The 'libel', lampoon or satire was a feature of Restoration court life as common as the love-song.

It could be simply a string of witty and usually bawdy insults in verse, but, in the hands of its ablest practitioners, notably Rochester, it became a vehicle for genuine social criticism based on a perception of the glaring contradictions between the smooth exterior of court life and the sordid actualities which lay behind it.

The Wits were a small, fairly closely knit community. Professor J. H. Wilson has estimated that about fourteen persons can be reckoned as belonging to the inner circle. As far as we know, they never authorized the printing of any of their works and a large quantity of their songs, 'libels' and other verses have survived in manuscript miscellanies, printed broadsides, contemporary anthologies, and editions, often of doubtful authenticity, published after their deaths. The result has been that it is extremely difficult for modern editors to establish either a reliable text or an authentic canon of the writings even of the leading figures.

As with the circle of Wyatt and Surrey in the early sixteenth century and that of the 'Sons of Ben Jonson' in the early seventeenth, there is a kind of basic poetic voice common to all the Restoration Wits who wrote verse. We can hear it in the following opening lines of a poem ascribed rather doubtfully to Dorset:

> Though, Phillis, your prevailing charms
> Have forc'd me from my Celia's arms,
> That kind defence against all powers,
> But those resistless eyes of yours:
> Think not your conquest to maintain
> By rigour and unjust disdain;
> In vain, fair Nymph, in vain you strive,
> For love does seldom hope survive . . .

This sort of rather thin, graceful poetry of conventional gallantry, strongly influenced by Waller and the slightly earlier French poetry of writers like Voiture and Sarrazin, could be written by almost any member of the circle including such minor poetasters as Lords Mulgrave and

Roscommon, Sir Car Scroop or Sir Fleetwood Shepherd. The 'most eminent wits', to use Burnet's expression, all sometimes make use of this 'basic' poetic voice but they are distinguished from their fellow courtiers by their power of speaking (or singing) in other voices covering wider and more interesting areas of experience.

II

JOHN WILMOT, EARL OF ROCHESTER

Rochester had by far the most powerful and original mind of all the Wits. His distinguishing characteristics are an unusual capacity for intellectual and sensual experience, a profound scepticism and a share in that quality of 'terrifying honesty' which T. S. Eliot ascribed to Blake. He began his career as a wholehearted disciple of Hobbes, but this was only the starting point for an intellectual voyage which ended with his conversion on his death bed to Christianity and his total rejection of what he then described as 'the absurd and foolish philosophy that the world so much admired, propagated by Mr. Hobbes and others'. In a letter to his wife he writes of 'so great a disproportion 'twixt our desires and what it has ordained to content them' and of those who are 'soe intirely satisfyed with theire shares in this world, that theire wishes nor their thoughts have not a farther prospect of felicity & glory'. One of his admirers called him an 'Enthusiast in Wit', and, if we interpret this as meaning that he combined intellectual toughness with a passionate aspiration to 'felicity and glory', the description is apt.

In the lyric he can play the game of the courtly pastoral and can also enjoy the fun of deflating its sentiment by substituting for the languishing swain and the chaste nymph a pair of cynical sensualists:

How perfect, Cloris, and how free
Would these enjoyments prove,
But you with formal jealousy
Are still tormenting Love.

Let us (since Wit instructs us how)
Raise pleasure to the top,
If Rival bottle you'll allow,
I'll suffer rival fop.

There's not a brisk insipid spark
That flutters in the Town
But with your wanton eyes you mark
Him out to be your own . . .

Such a poem as this is obviously a deliberate 'shocker'. We can hear in it the voice of the hard-boiled 'confident young men' who made people like the Duke of Ormonde shudder. J. M. Synge wrote in 1908 that 'before verse can become human again it must learn to be brutal'. These words can be applied to the age when seventeenth-century romanticism was dying as well as to that which saw the collapse of Victorian romanticism.

Rochester is writing from a far deeper level of experience in the following poem, where he gives a philosophic dimension to a favourite theme of the Wits, inconstancy:

LOVE AND LIFE

All my past Life is mine no more,
  The flying hours are gone:
Like transitory Dreams giv'n o're,
Whose Images are kept in store,
  By Memory alone.

The Time that is to come is not,
  How can it then be mine?
The present Moment's all my Lot,
And that, as fast as it is got,
  Phillis, is only thine.

Then talk not of Inconstancy,
  False Hearts, and broken Vows;

> If I, by Miracle, can be
> This live-long Minute true to thee,
>   'Tis all that Heav'n allows.

This attitude is very different from that of the thoughtless pleasure-seeker. The plangent cadences of the opening lines convey a sense of the mystery of the time-process and the whole poem is suffused with melancholy for the precariousness of the artificial paradise which the lover finds in the arms of his Phillis.

Rochester's break-through to reality in the lyric can take the form of passionate tenderness as well as brutality. This is found in a handful of lyrics which F. R. Leavis has well described as 'peculiarly individual utterances' and which were aptly compared by Sir Herbert Grierson to the songs of Burns:

> My dear Mistress has a Heart
>   Soft as those kind looks she gave me;
> When with Love's resistless Art,
>   And her Eyes she did enslave me,
> But her Constancy's so weak,
>   She's so wild, and apt to wander;
> That my jealous Heart wou'd break,
>   Should we live one day asunder.
>
> Melting Joys about her move,
>   Killing Pleasures, wounding Blisses;
> She can dress her Eyes in Love,
>   And her Lips can arm with Kisses.
> Angels listen when she speaks,
>   She's my delight, all Mankind's wonder:
> But my jealous Heart would break,
>   Should we live one day asunder.

Here the 'ease' and unaffected naturalness which the Wits prized are combined with a note of rapture and a crystalline perfection of phrase and form of which Rochester alone among them knew the secret.

His satiric poems are of two kinds. Some, like his attacks on Lord Mulgrave and Sir Car Scroop, are simply 'libels' in the fashion of the day and only distinguished from the numerous other contemporary squibs by their greater pungency and literary force. His lampoons on the king deserve special mention. The character of Charles II seems to have fascinated him, perhaps, because, like his own, it was full of paradoxes. The contrast between the traditional view of the monarch hedged by divinity and the actual person of the 'sauntering', informal Charles Stuart was a never-failing source of ironic amusement to the poet. It is neatly embodied in his celebrated extempore epigram:

> We have a pritty witty king
>   And whose word no man relys on:
> He never said a foolish thing,
>   And never did a wise one.

Charles's good-humoured reply is said to have been that what Rochester observed was easily explained. He was responsible for his words but his ministers for his actions. This epigram, however, is mild compared with some of the longer lampoons on the King ascribed to Rochester. What seemed to him especially despicable in the King was not that he took his pleasure with his mistresses but that he allowed himself to be governed by them:

> Restless he rolls about from Whore to Whore,
> A merry Monarch, scandalous and poor.

Rochester's more serious work in satire, however, deserves to be called philosophic; it can be seen as reflecting the dialectical process which transformed the gay young spark of the sixties into the dying penitent of 1680. One characteristic of these poems is his intense and vivid perception of the 'waste land' of the world revealed by the new materialistic philosophy together with the sordidness of a society vulgarized by the growth of the money power. The other is the creative use of his reading. He was the first poet to use the Augustan method of 'imitation', afterwards brilliantly exploited by Oldham, Pope and Johnson. Not only his fine

'Allusion to the Tenth Satire of the Second Book of Horace' but each of his major satiric works is at once a criticism of contemporary life and in some measure an 'imitation' or re-creation of a work of ancient or contemporary poetry often with a touch of parody. His famous lines 'Upon Nothing' are a kind of inversion of Cowley's 'Hymn to Light' and at the same time he makes use of the conception of Nothing as an active force found in the Renaissance Latin poems quoted by Johnson in his account of Rochester in *The Lives of the Poets;* behind the poem, too, lie still more august antecedents: the Book of Genesis, the first verses of the Fourth Gospel and the Aristotelian doctrine of form and matter:

> Nothing! thou Elder Brother ev'n to Shade,
> That hadst a Being e're the World was made,
> And (well fixt) art alone, of ending not afraid.

In the last stanzas the irony is transferred from metaphysics to contemporary society:

> Nothing who dwell'st with Fools in grave Disguise,
> For whom they rev'rend Shapes, and Forms devise,
> Lawn Sleeves and Furs and Gowns, when they like thee
>   look wise.

*   *   *   *

> The great Man's Gratitude to his best Friend,
> King's Promises, Whore's Vows, tow'rds thee they bend,
> Flow swiftly into thee, and in thee ever end.

The emptiness that lies behind the façade of human institutions and social life is visualized here as a kind of evil abstract deity (Blake's 'Nobodaddy'), and Swift's doctrine of man as a 'micro-coat' (see *A Tale of a Tub*) is clearly foreshadowed. Pope must have studied this poem carefully, for he wrote a clever imitation of it in his youth and the Triumph of Dullness at the end of *The Dunciad* probably owes much to Rochester's Triumph of Nothing.

'The Maim'd Debauchee', described by Charles Whibley as a 'masterpiece of heroic irony', recalls Davenant's epic

Gondibert as 'Upon Nothing' recalls Cowley's 'Hymn to Light'. The stately metre and diction of Davenant's 'heroic' poem are used to exhibit the old age of a gentlemanly rake, who is ironically equated to a superannuated admiral watching a naval battle from a safe position on shore. Like all Rochester's best satiric work this poem is not a statement but a vision. We are made to see the absurdly ferocious old sailor:

> From his fierce Eyes flashes of Rage he throws
>   As from black Clouds when Lightning breaks away,
> Transported thinks himself amidst his Foes,
>   And absent, yet enjoys the bloody Day.

This image is, as it were, superimposed upon that of the old *roué* inciting his young friends to the life of pleasure:

> My pains at last some respite shall afford,
>   While I behold the Battels you maintain:
> When Fleets of Glasses sail around the Board,
>   From whose Broad-Sides Volleys of Wit shall rain.

Are we looking at a riotous banquet or a naval battle? It is impossible to say; the two images are fused into a simple whole.

In his most powerful social satire 'A Letter from Artemisa in the Town to Cloe in the Country', Rochester shows us the obverse of the Utopia of Gallantry in which the Wits and ladies of Whitehall spent their time. In this poem the horror of the life of a prostitute in Restoration London is etched with the mordant realism of a Hogarth or a Goya:

> That wretched thing Corinna, who has run
> Through all the sev'ral ways of being undone:
> Cozen'd at first by Love, and living then
> By turning the too-dear-bought-cheat on Men:
> Gay were the hours, and wing'd with joy they flew,
> When first the Town her early Beauties knew:
> Courted, admir'd, and lov'd, with Presents fed;
> Youth in her Looks, and Pleasure in her bed.
>   ★ ★ ★

> Now scorn'd of all forsaken and opprest,
> She's a *Memento Mori* to the rest:
> Diseas'd, decay'd, to take up half a Crown
> Must Mortage her Long Scarf, and Manto Gown;
> Poor Creature, who unheard of, as a Flie,
> In some dark hole must all the Winter lye:
> And want, and dirt, endure a whole half year,
> That, for one month, she Tawdry may appear.

This is a glimpse of the hell over which the heaven of the Strephons and Cloes of Whitehall was precariously constructed.

The culmination of contemporary society is seen in his 'Satyr against Mankind', where the revolt is extended to an attack on the human condition itself. The poem was suggested by the eighth satire of Boileau, reinforced by hints from Montaigne and La Rochefoucauld. Nevertheless, it is a profoundly original work, for Rochester, like Pope, is never so original as when he is making full use of his reading. The poem is stamped with the peculiar strength of his personality in every line and expresses with an almost frightening intensity his mood of indignation and disillusionment. He never created a more striking image than that of mankind at the opening of the poem as the Lost Traveller, who, deceived by Reason, 'an *Ignis fatuus* in the Mind',

> Stumbling from thought to thought, falls head-long down
> Into doubts boundless Sea, where like to drown,
> Books bear him up awhile, and make him try,
> To swim with Bladders of Philosophy;
>
>   *   *   *
>
> Then Old Age, and experience, hand in hand,
> Lead him to death, and make him understand,
> After a search so painful, and so long,
> That all his Life he has been in the wrong;
> Hudled in dirt, the reas'ning Engine lyes,
> Who was so proud, so witty, and so wise.

Nowhere in the English poetry of the seventeenth century is the moral crisis of the age expressed with such force and precision; in the new mechanico-materialist universe of Descartes, Hobbes and the scientists, man is only a 'reas'ning Engine' (the phrase is probably suggested by an expression of Robert Boyle, the great contemporary chemist), yet the pitiful creature has the presumption to call himself witty and wise and seek an explanation of a universe in which he seems to be little better than an irrelevant accident. The central passage of the poem containing a comparison between man and the beasts is one of the most searching pieces of moral realism in English poetry:

> Be Judge your self, I'le bring it to the test,
> Which is the basest Creature Man or Beast?
> Birds feed on Birds, Beasts on each other prey,
> But Savage Man alone does Man betray:
> Prest by necessity, they Kill for Food,
> Man undoes Man to do himself no good.
> With Teeth and Claws by Nature arm'd they hunt,
> Nature's allowances, to supply their want;
> But Man with smiles, embraces, Friendships, praise,
> Unhumanely his Fellows life betrays;
> With voluntary pains works his distress,
> Not through necessity, but wantonness.
> For hunger, or for Love, they fight or tear,
> Whilst wretched Man is still in Arms for fear;
> For fear he arms, and is of Arms afraid,
> By fear, to fear, successively betray'd,
> Base fear, the source when his best passions came,
> His boasted Honor, and his dear bought Fame.
> That lust of Pow'r, to which he's such a Slave,
> And for the which alone he dares be brave . . .

Rochester is here piercing the defences of his aristocratic readers and showing the real passions that lay behind their highflown talk of 'Honor' and 'Fame'. It is a passage that communicates forward to the Swift of *Gulliver's Travels*: the King of Brobdingnag's denunciation of the Europeans and the superiority of those wise and humane quadrupeds, the Houyhnhnms to the filthy, cowardly Yahoos.

Rochester's reputation, like Byron's, has suffered from the blaze of notoriety which surrounded his life and personality. Andrew Marvell, no mean judge, declared that he was 'the best English satyrist and had the right veine', and Voltaire went further and called him 'a man of genius and a great poet'. As a craftsman in verse, compared with his contemporary John Dryden, he is a brilliant amateur. His place is among the daring thought-adventurers of English poetry, whose work lives by the intensity of their passion, the forthrightness of their speech and the searching clarity of their vision.

III

CHARLES SACKVILLE, EARL OF DORSET

Dorset (known throughout the early part of his career as Lord Buckhurst) was the least productive, though by no means the least gifted, of the Restoration Wits. The works which can be certainly attributed to him are a translation of one act of a tragedy of Corneille, a few lampoons, prologues and epilogues, a ribald parody, the well known ballad 'Song Written at Sea, in the first Dutch War' and a small sheaf of lyrics. He was rich and indolent and delighted in the company of men of letters, to whom he was a munificent host and patron. The condition of such a wealthy and universally flattered nobleman, 'fed', like Pope's Bufo, 'with soft dedication all day long', was perhaps even worse for a creative artist than the poverty and obscurity of an Oldham or an Otway. When Dryden couples his name with those of Virgil, Shakespeare and Donne, and Prior tells us that 'There is a Lustre in his Verses, like that of a Sun in Claude Loraine's Landskips' we are listening to the courtly hyperboles of the grateful recipients of his bounty. Pope, however, who was under no obligation to him, rated his poetry very highly, and if we can trust Spence's *Anecdotes*,

surprisingly preferred it even to Rochester's. His own work
shows that he studied it carefully.

Dorset's celebrated ballad deserves its reputation. An
excellent example of the benefit which the Wits derived
from their contact with the vernacular tradition, it is a true
street-ballad written to be sung to the traditional tune of
Shackerley Hay, and we know from the Stationer's Register
and Pepys's Diary (2 Jan. 1664/5) that it was actually published under the title of 'The Noble Seaman's Complaint'
as a broadside and was a popular hit. In this poem, as can be
judged from the following quotation of the three opening
stanzas, the rhythmic vitality of vernacular poetry is happily
combined with the sophisticated wit and irony of the
courtier, producing an effect that remains fresh and sparkling
after three centuries:

> To all you Ladies now at Land,
>   We Men at Sea indite;
> But first wou'd have you understand
>   How hard it is to write;
> The Muses now, and Neptune too,
> We must implore to write to you.
>
> For tho' the Muses should prove kind,
>   And fill our empty Brain;
> Yet if rough Neptune rouze the Wind,
>   To wave the azure Main,
> Our Paper, Pen and Ink, and we,
> Roll up and down our Ships at Sea.
>
> Then if we write not by each Post,
>   Think not we are unkind;
> Nor yet conclude our Ships are lost
>   By Dutchmen, or by Wind:
> Our Tears we'll send a speedier way,
> The Tide shall bring 'em twice a day.

Another lyric in the ballad style and metre has a touch of
the sturdy vulgarity and sensuality of popular art:

Methinks the poor Town has been troubled too long,
With Phillis and Chloris in every Song;
By Fools, who at once can both love and despair,
And will never leave calling 'em cruel and fair;
Which justly provokes me in Rhime to express
The Truth that I know of bonny black Bess.

This Bess of my Heart, this Bess of my Soul,
Has a Skin white as Milk and Hair black as Coal,
She's plump, yet with ease you may span her round Waste,
But her round swelling Thighs can scarce be embrac'd:
Her Belly is soft, not a word of the rest;
But I know what I think when I drink to the best.

The Plowman and 'Squire, the arranter Clown,
At home she subdu'd in her Paragon Gown;
But now she adorns the Boxes and Pit,
And the proudest Town-gallants are forc'd to submit;
All hearts fall a-leaping wherever she comes,
And beat Day and Night, like my Lord Craven's Drums.

Perhaps Dorset's most original and distinctive work is seen in the sequence of his four little poems on Katherine Sedley, the daughter of his friend Sir Charles. The character of this bold, witty young woman, who became the mistress of the Duke of York, afterwards James II, seems to have fascinated him. In these verses Dorset is creating a new kind of poem in which lyrical movement is combined with satiric force. It was, doubtless, of them that Rochester was thinking when he called him 'the best good Man, with the worst natur'd Muse'. The following poem has an economy of language and a classic perfection of form unrivalled in English poetry outside the works of Landor:

Dorinda's sparkling Wit and Eyes,
United, cast too fierce a Light,
Which blazes high, but quickly dies,
Pains not the Heart, but hurts the Sight.

Love is a calmer, gentler Joy.
Smooth are his Looks, and soft his Pace;

> Her Cupid is a black-guard Boy,
> That runs his Link full in your Face.

The metaphor of a painfully dazzling fire links the two
stanzas together with admirable art and the sudden transition
in the last two lines from the rococo cupid to the 'black-
guard Boy' with his flaming 'Link' (i.e. torch) takes us with
a pleasurable shock from the dreamworld of the pastoral
convention to the actuality of night in the murky streets of
Restoration London, where there were no street lamps and
the only illumination was provided by the torches of link-
boys. In another poem on Katherine Sedley the same verbal
economy and felicity of imagery gives force to a penetrating
piece of social satire:

> Tell me, Dorinda, why so gay,
>   Why such embroid'ry, fringe and lace?
> Can any Dresses find a way,
> To stop th' approaches of decay,
>   And mend a ruin'd Face.
>
> Wilt thou still sparkle in the Box,
>   Still ogle in the Ring?
> Canst thou forget thy Age and Pox?
> Can all that shines on Shells and Rocks
>   Make thee a fine young Thing?
>
> So have I seen in Larder dark
>   Of Veal a lucid Loin
> Replete with many a brilliant Spark,
> As wise Philosophers remark,
>   At once both stink and shine.

This is not merely an attack on Katherine Sedley. It is a
dramatization of a true social criticism which sees all the
glittering apparatus of court life ('embroid'ry, fringe and
lace' and 'all that shines on Shells and Rocks') as a mockery
masking the hideous realities of venereal disease and decaying
flesh. There is a sharp visualization of ugly and sordid
images in this poem revealing a new kind of poetic sensibility
which was to be exploited with remarkable results by Pope

and Swift. A similar quality is found in one of Dorset's lampoons on the Hon. Edward Howard, a contemporary dramatist who was one of the favourite butts of the Wits:

Thou damn'd Antipodes to Common sense,
Thou Foil to Flecknoe, pry'thee tell from whence
Does all this mighty Stock of Dullness spring?
Is it thy own, or hast it from Snow-Hill,
Assisted by some Ballad-making Quill?
No, they fly higher yet, thy Plays are such
I'd swear they were translated out of Dutch,
Fain wou'd I know what Diet thou dost keep,
If thou dost always, or dost never sleep?
Sure hasty-pudding is thy chiefest Dish,
With Bullock's Liver, or some stinking Fish;
Garbage, Ox-cheeks, and Tripes, do feast thy Brain
Which nobly pays this tribute back again,
With Daisy roots thy dwarfish Muse is fed,
A Giant's body with a Pygmy's head.

* * *

Think on't a while, and thou wilt quickly find
Thy Body made for Labour, not thy Mind.
No other use of Paper thou should'st make,
Than carrying Loads and Reams upon thy Back.
Carry vast Burdens till thy Shoulders shrink,
But curst be he that gives thee Pen and Ink:
Such dang'rous Weapons shou'd be kept from Fools,
As Nurses from their children keep Edg'd-Tools:
For thy dull Fancy a Muckinder[1] is fit
To wipe the slabberings of thy snotty Wit.

Dr. Johnson rightly saw in these lines evidence of 'great fertility of mind'. They show a strength and a freedom of imagination which make us think of *The Dunciad* and regret that Dorset's birth and fortune prevented him from developing his considerable literary potentiality.

---

[1] Muckinder=a handkerchief.

IV

SIR CHARLES SEDLEY

Pope described Sedley as 'a very insipid writer; except in some few of his little love-verses'. This is not quite fair to Sedley, who wrote some good poetry besides his 'little love verses', but it is possible to understand what Pope meant. Sedley's poetry has neither Rochester's passionate intensity and intellectual energy nor the satiric bite and sensuality of Dorset's best work. He uses the old stereotypes of the courtly pastoral convention with grace and wit, sometimes with tenderness, but rarely with passion. His attitude to the sex-relationship is rational and humorous:

> Phillis, let's shun the common Fate
> And let our Love ne'r turn to Hate.
> I'll dote no longer than I can
> Without being call'd a faithless Man.
> When we begin to want Discourse
> And Kindness seems to taste of Force,
> As freely as we met we'll part
> Each one possest of his own Heart.

In two poems he uses the theme of the address to a very young girl, treated already with imaginative richness by Marvell and courtly grace by Waller. The following are the opening stanzas of the song to Cloris in Sedley's comedy, *The Mulberry Garden:*

> Ah Cloris! that I now could sit
>   As unconcern'd as when
> Your Infant Beauty cou'd beget
>   No pleasure, nor no pain.
>
> When I the Dawn us'd to admire,
>   And prais'd the coming Day;
> I little thought the growing fire
>   Must take my Rest away.

> Your Charms in harmless Childhood lay,
>   Like metals in the mine,
> Age from no face took more away,
>   Than Youth conceal'd in thine.
>
> But as your Charms insensibly
>   To their perfection prest,
> Fond Love as unperceiv'd did flye
>   And in my Bosom rest.
>
> My passion with your Beauty grew,
>   And Cupid at my heart,
> Still as his mother favour'd you,
>   Threw a new flaming Dart.

This is, perhaps, a little too pretty. It might be described a boudoir poetry, recalling some erotic French eighteenth-century painting of the school of Boucher. More astringent and satisfying to a modern taste in its delicate, playful humour is the poem addressed 'To a Devout Young Gentlewoman':

> Phillis, this early Zeal asswage,
>   You over-act your part;
> The Martyrs, at your tender Age,
>   Gave Heaven but half their Heart.
>
> Old Men (till past the Pleasure) ne're
>   Declaim against the Sin;
> 'Tis early to begin to fear
>   The Devil at Fifteen.
>
> The World to Youth is too severe,
>   And, like a treacherous Light,
> Beauty, the Actions of the Fair,
>   Exposes to their sight.
>
> And yet the World, as old as 'tis,
>   Is oft deceiv'd by't too;
> Kind Combinations seldom miss,
>   Let's try what we can do.

The first two stanzas of this poem are nearly flawless but the last two are marred both by banality of thought and

verbal clumsiness, seen in the awkward inversions and the
slipshod grammar of the penultimate stanza. A similar
failure of inspiration mars the lyric beginning with the
following often-praised and beautiful lines:

> Love still has something of the Sea,
> From whence his Mother rose;

The expectation aroused by this rich opening is immediately
damped by the next two lines with their hackneyed imagery
and inversion for the sake of the rhyme:

> No time his Slaves from Doubt can free,
> Nor give their Thoughts repose

After a series of stanzas filled with frigid allegory the
poems ends with lines almost worthy of its superb opening:

> And if I gaz'd a thousand Years
> I could no deeper love.

None of the weaknesses noted in these poems is found in
two of Sedley's songs which for long retained their popu-
larity through the contemporary musical settings. In the
following poem the courtly convention is most happily
wedded to the appreciation of an exquisite moment of
actual experience:

> Hears not my Phillis, how the Birds
>   Their feather'd Mates salute?
> They tell their Passion in their Words;
>   Must I alone be mute?
> Phillis, without Frown or Smile,
> Sat and knotted all the while.
>
> The God of Love in thy bright Eyes
>   Does like a Tyrant reign;
> But in thy Heart a Child he lyes,
>   Without his Dart or Flame.
> Phillis, without Frown or Smile,
> Sat and knotted all the while.

So many Months in Silence past,
   And yet in raging Love,
Might well deserve one Word at last
   My Passion shou'd approve.
Phillis, without Frown or Smile,
Sat and knotted all the while.

Must then your faithful Swain expire,
   And not one look obtain,
Which he to sooth his fond Desire
   Might pleasingly explain?
Phillis, without Frown or Smile,
Sat and knotted all the while.

This lyric must be heard sung to Purcell's exquisite setting if
its full effect is to be realized, but even on the printed page it
succeeds in conveying the poet's delight in the ballet-like
situation, in the movement of the verse and the conventional
images, which his emotion endows with a surprising freshness and vitality. Equally successful is an even more famous
song which shows an originality of metrical invention
unusual in Sedley's work and due, doubtless, in some measure
to the music:

Phillis is my only Joy,
   Faithless as the Winds or Seas;
Sometimes coming, sometimes coy,
   Yet she never fails to please;
      If with a Frown
      I am cast down,
      Phillis smiling,
      And beguiling,
Makes me happier than before.

Tho', alas, too late I find,
   Nothing can her Fancy fix;
Yet the Moment she is kind,
   I forgive her all her Tricks;
      Which tho' I see,
      I can't get free;

> She deceiving,
> I believing;
> What need Lovers wish for more?

In one lyric Sedley achieves the expression of tender feeling in language of diaphanous simplicity that almost equals that of Rochester's best songs, though, as so often in his poetry, the magnificent promise of the opening lines is hardly sustained:

> Not, Celia, that I juster am
>   Or better than the rest,
> For I would change each Hour like them,
>   Were not my heart at rest.
>
> But I am ty'd to very thee
>   By every Thought I have,
> Thy Face I only crave to see,
>   Thy Heart I only crave.
>
> All that in Woman is ador'd
>   In thy dear self I find,
> For the whole Sex can but afford
>   The Handsome and the kind.
>
> Why then should I seek farther Store,
>   And still make Love anew?
> When Change itself can give no more,
>   'Tis easie to be true.

Sedley is not, however, exclusively what Ben Jonson calls 'a woman's poet'. There is a more masculine quality in some of the poems probably written in the later part of his life. This quality is found especially in his translations and imitations of Latin poetry. Prior with true critical insight described him as 'Sir Charles that can write and better Translate'. His version of the eighth Ode of the Second Book of Horace is one of the finest verse translations of the seventeenth century. It is one of those rare translations that reads like an original poem. Horace's dangerous old harlot is transmuted into one of the glittering, rapacious courtesans of the Court of

Charles II and the poem is as vivid, incisive and carefully controlled as the Latin original:

> Did any Punishment attend
>   Thy former Perjuries
> I should believe a second time
>   Thy charming Flatteries:
> Did but one Wrinkle mark this Face,
> Or hadst thou lost one single Grace.
>
> No sooner hast thou, with false Vows,
>   Provok'd the Powers above;
> But thou art fairer than before
>   And we are more in love.
> Thus Heaven and Earth seem to declare,
> They pardon Falshood in the Fair.
>
> Sure 'tis no Crime vainly to swear,
>   By ev'ry Power on high,
> And call our bury'd Mother's Ghost
>   A witness to the Lye:
> Heaven at such Perjuries connives,
> And Venus with a Smile forgives.
>
> The Nymphs and cruel Cupid too,
>   Sharp'ning his pointed Dart
> On an old hone besmear'd with Blood,
>   Forbear thy perjur'd Heart.
> Fresh Youth grows up, to wear thy Chains,
> And the Old Slave no Freedom gains.
>
> Thee, Mothers for their eldest Sons,
>   Thee, wretched Misers fear,
> Lest thy prevailing Beauty should
>   Seduce the hopeful Heir.
> New-marry'd Virgins fear thy Charms
> Should keep their Bridegroom from their Arms.

A similar strength is found in a series of adaptations of epigrams of Martial, one of the best of which is cast in the form of a Shakespearian sonnet and must be one of the very few poems in this form written between the early seventeenth and early nineteenth centuries:

> Thou art an Atheist, Quintus, and a Wit,
>   Thinkst all was of self-moving Attoms made,
> Religion only for the Vulgar fit,
>   Priests Rogues, and Preaching their deceitful Trade;
> Wilt drink, whore, fight, blaspheme, damn, curse and swear:
>   Why wilt thou swear by God, if there be none?
> And if there be, thou shouldst his Vengeance fear:
>   Methinks this Huffing might be let alone;
> 'Tis thou art free, Mankind besides a Slave,
>   And yet a Whore can lead thee by the Nose,
> A drunken Bottle, and a flatt'ring Knave,
>   A mighty Prince, Slave to thy dear Soul's Foes,
> Thy Lust, thy Rage, Ambition and thy Pride;
> He that serves God, need nothing serve beside.

This poem shows that Sedley was capable not only of living in the libertine 'Utopia of Gallantry' but of outgrowing it and criticizing it, though his criticism lacks the philosophic depth and fierce irony of Rochester's.

At the end of his life he wrote a long poem on marriage called 'The Happy Pair'. In spite of some rather banal theorizing, the passages denouncing mercenary and loveless marriages have a note of actuality due, no doubt, to the poet's own bitter experience; he was married at the age of seventeen to a woman who became a paranoiac. The conclusion of the poem with its praise of quiet domesticity shows that the wild gallant of the sixteen-sixties had by the end of the century developed into an Augustan 'man of feeling'. In the following lines there is a sensuous perception of 'images of external nature' which foreshadows the rural-sentimental poetry of the eighteenth century:

> Love, like a cautious fearful Bird, ne'er builds,
> But where the Place Silence and Calmness yields:
> He slily flies to Copses, where he finds
> The snugging Woods secure from Blasts and Winds,
> Shuns the huge Boughs of a more Stately Form,
> And Laughs at Trees tore up with ev'ry Storm.

V

SIR GEORGE ETHEREGE

Unlike the other members of the Court circle Etherege did not come from a wealthy, aristocratic background. His grandfather was a 'vintner', or publican, at Maidenhead and his father, after spending some time in the Bermudas, held a small appointment at the Court of Charles I and died in exile in France after the royalist defeat. The only fact that we know about the young George Etherege is that he was apprenticed by his grandfather to a London attorney in 1653 at the age of eighteen. Eleven years later his first play was produced with great success at the Duke's Theatre; he dedicated it to Lord Buckhurst (Dorset) and there is no doubt that it was through his friendship with that nobleman that he was accepted as a member of the 'merry gang'. This experience was the central fact of his life. Like Oscar Wilde two centuries later, he was a wit and an artist in comedy, who was admitted into aristocratic circles, and was enchanted by the ideal of the man of fashion and leisure who was master of the art of living. In each of his three comedies we find this figure, beginning with the sketch of the gay and charming Sir Frederick Frollick in *The Comical Revenge*, proceeding to the two attractive young sparks, Courtall and Freeman, in *She Wou'd If She Cou'd* and culminating in the finished portrait of Dorimant in *The Man of Mode*, said to be based on the character of Rochester. Contrasted with Dorimant in this play is Sir Fopling Flutter, that 'eminent Coxcomb', who embodies all that is absurd in the fashionable ideal. Etherege himself was probably something halfway between Dorimant and Sir Fopling. Just as Wilde called himself a *poseur*, so Etherege called himself a fop. In one of his letters he writes: 'I confess I am a fop in my heart; ill customs influence my senses, and I have been so used to affection [affectation] that without the air of the Court nothing can touch me'. Unlike the other members of the

merry gang he never outgrew the courtly-libertine ideal of
the sixteen-sixties. Like Wilde he was never so much himself
as when he was acting a part and the part of the 'fop' or perfect aesthetic hero became second nature to him. It might be
imagined that such a man, when he wrote verse, would speak
only in the 'basic voice' of the court poet. Actually, however,
in Etherege's poetry, slight as it is in quantity, we can hear
other and more individual voices. John Palmer acutely
ascribed to him 'a worldly simplicity captivating from its
entire lack of self-consciousness' and this describes very well
the quality of his best lyrics. His poem addressed 'To a very
Young Lady' has none of the playfulness and boudoir
eroticism of Sedley's 'Song to Cloris' but a kind of innocent
freshness which brings him nearer to Marvell or even
Vaughan than to Waller or Sedley:

> Sweetest bud of beauty, may
> No untimely frost decay
> The early glories that we trace,
> Blooming in thy matchless face;
> But kindly opening, like the rose,
> Fresh beauties every day disclose,
> Such as by nature are not shown
> In all the blossoms she has blown—
> And then what conquest shall you make
> Who hearts already daily take?
> Scorched in the morning with thy beams,
> How shall we bear those sad extremes
> Which must attend thy threatening eyes
> When thou shalt to thy noon arise.

The following lyric is more characteristic. Here the voice is
that of a *persona*, the 'shepherd' or ideal poet of the court
pastoral, a fairy tale or tapestry world. The attitude of the
'shepherd', we may notice, is highly ambiguous. Ostensibly
he is issuing a warning against the love of women, but we
are told that love's 'chain' is 'imperial' and its 'pain'
'enchanting', and it seems obvious that the loss of 'quiet' by

those who gaze on 'beauteous Eyes' is a not unenviable
condition:

> Ye happy youths, whose hearts are free
>   From Love's imperial chain,
> Henceforth be warned and taught by me
>   T'avoid the enchanting pain.
> Fatal the wolves to trembling flocks,
>   Sharp winds to blossoms prove,
> To careless seamen hidden rocks,
>   To human quiet Love.
>
> Fly the fair sex if bliss you prize,
>   The snake's beneath the flower;
> Whoever gazed on beauteous eyes
>   That tasted quiet more?
> How faithless is the lover's joy!
>   How constant is his care!
> The kind with falsehood do destroy,
>   The cruel with despair.

The craftsmanship of this poem is remarkable. The common
ballad quatrain is enlivened by a subtle pattern of alliteration
and assonance and the cadences ('human quiet Love', 'gazed
on beauteous eyes', 'tasted quiet more') are the work of a
fine artist in verbal music. He is equally successful with
flowing anapaests in the song called 'Silvia'. Here the
feeling is genuine but it is of the kind that can be called
operatic like that of Tom Moore's best songs, the manner
of which is remarkably foreshadowed in this poem. It is
interesting to find that it was immensely popular as 'words
for music' and was set by no fewer than four different
contemporary composers:

> The nymph that undoes me is fair and unkind,
> No less than a wonder by Nature designed;
> She's the grief of my heart, the joy of my eye,
> And the cause of a flame that never can die.
>
> Her mouth, from whence wit still obligingly flows
> Has the beautiful blush and the smell of the rose;

Love and destiny both attend on her well,
She wounds with a look, with a frown she can kill.

The desperate lover can hope no redress
Where beauty and rigor are both in excess:
In Silvia they meet, so unhappy am I,
Who sees her must love and who loves her must die.

Etherege can speak in other voices in his poetry besides that
of the courtly gallant. In some of the lyrics in his plays we
can hear the voice of the man of the street, the tavern and
the coffee-house, using the idiom of the popular song, catch
and street-ballad. The following lines, trolled by the sharper
Palmer in the tavern scene in *The Comical Revenge* (II. 2),
have the salty tang of vernacular speech and the hearty
sensuality of popular poetry:

If she be not fair as kind
    But peevish and unhandy,
Leave her—she's only worth the care
    Of some spruce Jack-a-dandy.

I would not have thee such an ass,
    Hadst thou ne'er so much leisure
To sigh and whine for such a lass
    Whose pride's above her pleasure.

Make much of every buxom girl
    Which needs but little courting;
Her value is above the pearl,
    That takes delight in sporting.

The song sung by the 'wanton' Gatty in the first scene of the
fifth act of *She Wou'd If She Cou'd* is a genuine street-ballad
which was reprinted in two broadsides. It is poetry that
springs as directly from the life of Restoration London as an
entry in Pepys's Diary:

To little or no purpose I spent many days,
In ranging the Park, the Exchange, and the Plays;
For ne'er in my rambles till now did I prove
So lucky to meet with the man I could love.

Oh! how I am pleased when I think on this man,
That I find I must love, let me do what I can!

How long I shall love him, I can no more tell
Than had I a fever when I should be well.
My passion shall kill me before I will show it,
And yet I would give all the world he did know it;
But oh how I sigh when I think he would woo me,
I cannot deny what I know would undo me.

As a poet Etherege is seen at his best in his lyrics; his few
complimentary and erotic poems in the heroic couplet are
polished but undistinguished. His lines to the Marchioness of
Newcastle 'after the Reading of Her Incomparable Poems'
might have been written by any competent imitator of
Waller:

Those graces nature did till now divide
(Your sex's glory and our sex's pride)
Are joined in you, and all to you submit,
The brightest beauty and the sharpest wit.
No faction here or fiercer envy sways,
They give you myrtle, while we offer bays.
What mortal dares dispute this wreath with you,
Armed thus with lightning and with thunder too.

He is said to have written lampoons railing at women, but
no 'libel' can be certainly ascribed with him. If he is the
author of 'Mrs Nelly's Complaint', a satire on Nell Gwynn
attributed to him in *The Miscellaneous Works of the Duke of
Buckingham*, he cannot be credited with a satiric talent
beyond that of those whom Dryden calls 'our common
libellers'. The best passage in the poem gives an amusing
glimpse of the strangely variegated company that was to
be found in the royal presence at Whitehall in the reign of
Charles II:

Let mountebanks make market houses ring
Of what great feats they've done before the King,
Let learned Sir Sam his Windsor Engine try,
Before great Charles let quacks and seamen lie.

> He ne'er heard swearers till Mall Knight and I,
> Never heard oaths less valued, or less true
> (And yet 'tis said, he has paid for swearing too)
> Loudlier we swore than plundering dragoons,
> 'Sblood followed 'Sblood, and Zoons succeeded Zoons.

A more individual note is heard in a series of verse epistles written by Etherege to his friends in the tumbling four accent 'Hudibrastic' metre popularized by Butler's famous poem. In this metre he conducted a witty but obscene correspondence with Buckhurst and, later, when he was British Envoy at Ratisbon, wrote verse epistles to his friend and official superior Lord Middleton. One of these epistles contains a description of one of 'rough Danube's beauties' which combines the picturesque with the comic in a manner that Byron would not have despised:

> How would the ogling sparks despise
> The darling damsel of my eyes,
> Did they behold her at a play,
> As she's tricked up on holiday,
> When the whole family combine
> For public pride to make her shine.
> Her hair which long before lay matted
> Are on this day combed out and platted
> A diamond bodkin in each tress
> The badges of her nobleness;
> For every stone as well as she
> Can boast an ancient pedigree.
>   *   *   *   *
> No serpent breaking in the air
> Can with her starry head compare.
> Such ropes of pearls her hands encumber
> She scarce can deal the cards at ombre;
> So many rings each finger freight,
> They tremble with the mighty weight:
> The like in England ne'er was seen
> Since Holbein drew Hal and his Queen.
> But after these fantastic sights
> The luster's meaner than the lights

> She that bears this glittering pomp
> Is but a tawdry ill-bred ramp
> Whose brawny limbs and martial face
> Proclaim her of the Gothic race,
> More than the painted pageantry
> Of all her father's heraldry . . .

Unlike the other 'eminent wits' Etherege never goes beneath the surface in his poetry. It is all 'light verse' but, at the same time, it is the work of a true artist and it succeeds in transmitting across three centuries his gaiety, insouciance and attractive mixture of innocence and sophistication.

VI

CONCLUSION

The pattern of life and writing of the 'merry gang' arose from a particular phase of society and culture and could not be repeated. Men like George Granville, Lord Lansdowne and William Walsh, who tried to reproduce it after the Revolution, appear now as Young Pretenders, mere pale and colourless imitations. By the end of the century the character of the libertine Court Wit had become the absurd anachronism which Swift caricatures in *A Tale of A Tub* when he describes the activities of the three brothers in high society: 'they writ and rallied, and rhymed and sung and said, and said nothing: they drank and fought, and slept, and swore, and took snuff: they went to new plays on the first night, haunted the chocolate houses, beat the watch, lay on bulks, and got claps: they bilked hackney-coachmen, ran in debt with shopkeepers, and lay with their wives: they killed bailiffs, kicked fidlers downstairs, eat at Will's, loitered at Locket's . . .'. The men who did these things in Swift's time were, to use his own expression, mere micro-coats, imitators of the externals of what had once been a life of gaiety, poetry and adventure. Alone among men of the post-Revolution generation William Congreve caught the authentic note of the Restoration Wits in a few poems such as the following lyric, the first stanza of which, at least, Rochester would not have disowned:

> False though she be to me and love,
>   I'll ne'er pursue revenge;
> For still the charmer I approve
>   Though I deplore her change.
>
> In hours of bliss we oft have met,
>   They could not always last;
> For though the present I regret,
>   I'm grateful for the past.

The best of the poetry of the Wits lives to-day by virtue of its youthfulness, insouciance, direct and unaffected speech, irreverence and sensuality. These qualities are, perhaps, more acceptable now than at any time since the latter part of the seventeenth century. For long the aura of scandal surrounding the personalities of the Wits obscured the historical significance of their writings. They rendered two great services to English poetry. One was to keep the singing voice of the lyric alive in an age of mathematics and scientific positivism. Boileau said that Descartes had cut the throat of poetry. It was to a large extent due to the 'merry gang' that the positive spirit of Descartes, Hobbes and the scientists failed to cut the throat of the English lyric. Their other memorable achievement was to diversify and invigorate the Augustan tradition by preserving the happy freedom of colloquial, informal English poetry, a heritage which they handed on to the Queen Anne Wits, Swift, Pope, Prior and Gay, and through them to the Byron of 'Beppo', 'The Vision of Judgment' and 'Don Juan'.

THE RESTORATION COURT POETS

A Select Bibliography

(Books published in London, unless otherwise stated)

Abbreviations

CHEL   *Cambridge History of English Literature*
ESMEA   *Essays and Studies by Members of the English Association*
MLN   *Modern Language Notes*
NQ   *Notes and Queries*
PQ   *Philological Quarterly*
RES   *Review of English Studies*
RMS   *Renaissance and Modern Studies*

JOHN WILMOT, EARL OF ROCHESTER

Bibliography:

JOHN WILMOT, EARL OF ROCHESTER, HIS LIFE AND WRITINGS, by J. Prinz.
Leipzig (1927)
—contains a full descriptive bibliography of Rochester's writings.
ROCHESTER'S POEMS ON SEVERAL OCCASIONS, ed. J. Thorpe. Princeton
(1950)
—deals with the complex status and order of the so-called 'Antwerp'
editions (see below). This and the following work contain valuable
bibliographical information not in Prinz.
ATTRIBUTION IN RESTORATION POETRY, by D. Vieth (1963).

Collected Works:

POEMS ON SEVERAL OCCASIONS. 'Antwerp' (1680)
—the 'Antwerp' imprint is almost certainly spurious. At least ten
editions (fewer than twenty copies of which have survived) were
surreptitiously printed from 1680 onwards, either dated or ante-
dated 1680, or without date. It includes a number of poems which
are not by Rochester. A facsimile of the Huntington Library copy,
ed. J. Thorpe, Princeton, 1950, contains a valuable introduction and
notes.

POEMS ON SEVERAL OCCASIONS (1685)

—omits nine poems which appeared in the preceding collection but adds five others. Reprinted, 1701, 1712.

POEMS &C. ON SEVERAL OCCASIONS, WITH VALENTINIAN, A TRAGEDY (1691)

—an expurgated text but contains additional authentic poems. Published by Jacob Tonson with Preface by Thomas Rymer. Reprinted, 1696, 1705.

THE MISCELLANEOUS WORKS (1707)

—printed and sold by B. Bragge. Pirated by E. Curll, 1707, 1709. Contains poems by other authors besides Rochester. The 'Life of Rochester' is not (as stated in the title) by Saint Evremond.

THE WORKS (1714)

—a reprint of Tonson's edition of 1705 including a number of Rochester's letters. For later editions, notably of the 2-vol. collection of poems by Rochester, Roscommon, Dorset, &c., 1714 (many times reprinted with or without 'The Cabinet of Love' appendix during the 18th century), see Prinz's bibliography.

THE COLLECTED WORKS, ed. J. Hayward (1926)

—contains almost everything that has been attributed to Rochester, including a number of spurious poems. A Nonesuch limited edition.

POEMS, ed. V. de S. Pinto (1953)

—in the Muses' Library. The first attempt to establish a reliable canon, though not a definitive text, of the poems. Includes an appendix of poems attributed to Rochester on doubtful authority. Revised edition, 1964.

Separate Works:

A SATYR AGAINST MANKIND WRITTEN BY A PERSON OF HONOUR [c.1679]

—a folio poem published according to Anthony à Wood in June 1679. Several of Rochester's poems were published separately in folio towards the end of his life (v., as examples, the two following entries).

UPON NOTHING BY A PERSON OF HONOUR [c.1679]

—two undated folios published about 1679. Reprinted by E. Curll, 1711, and by R. H. Griffiths, Texas, 1946.

A LETTER FROM ARTEMISA IN THE TOWN TO CHLOE IN THE COUNTRY (1670, also undated)

—two editions in folio exist.

VALENTINIAN A TRAGEDY AS 'TIS ALTER'D BY THE LATE EARL OF ROCHESTER (1685—two issues)

—contains an important preface by Robert Wolseley, reprinted in *Critical Essays of the Seventeenth Century*, edited by J. E. Spingarn, vol. iii, 1909.

FAMILIAR LETTERS. 2 vols. (1697 *bis*)

—reprinted 1699, 1705.

THE ROCHESTER-SAVILE LETTERS 1671-1680, ed. J. H. Wilson. Columbus, Ohio (1941)

—a modern edition of the letters to Henry Savile in *Familiar Letters* together with Savile's extant letters to Rochester.

THE FAMOUS PATHOLOGIST OR THE NOBLE MOUNTEBANK, by Thomas Alcock and John Wilmot Earl of Rochester, ed. V. de S. Pinto. Nottingham (1961)

—Rochester's 'Mountebank Bill' printed from the MS of his servant T. Alcock with Alcock's preface telling how he masqueraded as the Italian quack doctor 'Bendo'. A contemporary, possibly the original, printed edition of Alexander Bendo's Advertisement (no place, printer, or date) has survived in an apparently unique copy.

Some Biographical and Critical Studies:

A SERMON PREACHED AT THE FUNERAL OF THE RT. HONORABLE JOHN EARL OF ROCHESTER, by R. Parsons. Oxford (1680)

SOME PASSAGES OF THE LIFE AND DEATH OF THE RIGHT HONOURABLE JOHN EARL OF ROCHESTER, by G. Burnet (1680)

—reprinted in numerous 18th-century editions (and in *English Biography of the Seventeenth Century*, edited by V. de S. Pinto, 1951), and the basis of many hortatory tracts and pious pamphlets issued as religious propaganda up to the end of the 19th century.

THE LIVES OF THE MOST EMINENT ENGLISH POETS, by S. Johnson (1781)

—includes Johnson's Life of Rochester.

'John Wilmot Comte de Rochester', par E. D. Forgues. In *La Revue de Deux Mondes*, Aug.-Sept. 1857.

ROCHESTERIANA, collected and edited by J. Prinz. Leipzig (1926).

JOHN WILMOT, EARL OF ROCHESTER, HIS LIFE AND WRITINGS, by J. Prinz. Leipzig (1927).

ROCHESTER, by C. Williams (1935).

BEAST IN VIEW, by F. Whitfield. Cambridge, Mass. (1939).

'Rochester and the Right Veine of Satire', by V. de S. Pinto. In *ESMEA*, N.S. v, 1953.

'Rochester's "Scepter Lampoon" on Charles II', by D. Vieth. In *PQ*, 37, 1958.

'Rochester and Dryden', by V. de S. Pinto. In *RMS*, v, 1961.

ENTHUSIAST IN WIT: A PORTRAIT OF JOHN WILMOT EARL OF ROCHESTER, by V. de S. Pinto (1962)

—revised and enlarged edition of *Rochester: Portrait of a Restoration Poet*, by the same author, 1935.

CHARLES SACKVILLE, EARL OF DORSET

Bibliography:

'A Check-List of Dorset's Poems', by H. A. Bagley. In *MLN*, xlvii, November 1932, pp. 454-61.

'Some Additions to the Poems of Lord Dorset', by R. G. Howarth. In *MLN*, l, November 1935, p. 457.

Collected Works:

THE WORKS OF THE EARLS OF ROCHESTER, ROSCOMMON, DORSET &C. 2 vols. (1714)

—vol. ii contains the earliest known collection of 'Poems by the Earl of Dorset'.

THE WORKS OF THE MOST CELEBRATED MINOR POETS. 2 vols. (1749)

—vol. i contains 'Poems by the Earl of Dorest'. Reprinted Dublin, 1751.

A SUPPLEMENT TO THE WORKS OF THE MINOR POETS PART I (n.d.)

—contains additional poems by Dorset.

Separate Works:

POMPEY THE GREAT (1664)

—translation of *La Mort de Pompée* of P. Corneille. See below under 'Sir Charles Sedley'.

THE NOBLE SEAMANS COMPLAINT TO THE LADIES AT LAND TO YE TUNE OF SHACKERLEY HAY

—broadside ballad entered in the Stationers' Register, 30 December 1664. No copy is known to survive. This is Dorset's famous ballad usually known as 'Song Written at Sea in the First Dutch War'. The earliest extant printed version is that which appears in *Wit and Mirth or Pills to Purge Melancholy*, Vol. V, 1714, pp. 168-70 under the title 'A Ballad by the Late Lord Dorset when at Sea'. There is an early manuscript version of this poem in Br. Mus. Harl. MS 3991, printed by N. Ault in his *Seventeenth Century Lyrics*, 1928, p. 333.

A COLLECTION OF POEMS WRITTEN UPON SEVERAL OCCASIONS BY SEVERAL PERSONS (1672)
—printed for Hobart Kemp. Contains three poems probably by Buckhurst (Dorset). This important collection was the predecessor or a number of other Restoration miscellanies containing a few poems by Dorset.

POEMS ON AFFAIRS OF STATE (1697)
—contains Dorset's 'The Duel of the Crabs', a parody of Sir Robert Howard's 'The Duel of the Stags'.

Some Biographical and Critical Studies:

THE LIVES OF THE MOST EMINENT ENGLISH POETS, by S. Johnson (1781)
—includes Johnson's Life of Dorset.

CHARLES SACKVILLE, SIXTH EARL OF DORSET PATRON AND POET OF THE RESTORATION, by B. Harris. Urbana, Illinois (1940).

SIR CHARLES SEDLEY

Bibliography:

THE POETICAL AND DRAMATIC WORKS, ed. V. de S. Pinto. 2 vols. (1928)
—contains a bibliography of Sedley's writings.

Collected Works:

THE MISCELLANEOUS WORKS, ed. Capt. Ayloffe (1702)
—reprinted with additional material, not all of which is by Sedley, 1707 and 1710.

THE WORKS, 2 vols. (1722)
—contains an account of the Life of Sedley, possibly by Defoe. Reprinted, 1776 and 1778.

THE POETICAL AND DRAMATIC WORKS, ed. V. de S. Pinto. 2 vols. (1928).

Separate Works:

POMPEY THE GREAT (1664)
—translation of *La Mort de Pompée* of P. Corneille by Waller, Buckhurst, Sedley, Godolphin and Filmer. Act III possibly by Sedley.

THE MULBERRY GARDEN (1668)
—reprinted, 1675 and 1688.

A COLLECTION OF POEMS WRITTEN UPON SEVERAL OCCASIONS BY SEVERAL PERSONS (1672)
—printed for Hobart Kemp. Contains about thirty poems by Sedley, including some of his best lyrics. Reprinted for T. Collins and

J. Ford, 1673. Contains some additional matter. Reprinted with further additional matter and some alterations for F. Saunders, 1693.

ANTONY AND CLEOPATRA (1677)

—reprinted, 1696.

BELLAMIRA OR THE MISTRESS (1687).

THE HAPPY PAIR (1702)

Biographical and Critical Study:

SIR CHARLES SEDLEY, by V. de S. Pinto (1927).

SIR GEORGE ETHEREGE

Bibliography:

THE DRAMATIC WORKS, ed. H. F. B. Brett Smith. 2 vols. Oxford (1927)

—contains a bibliography of the plays.

THE POEMS, ed. J. Thorpe. Princeton (1963)

—contains valuable bibliographical information about the poems.

Collected Works:

THE WORKS (1704).

THE WORKS, ed. A. W. Verity (1888).

THE DRAMATIC WORKS, ed. H. F. B. Brett Smith. 2 vols. Oxford (1927).

THE POEMS, ed. J. Thorpe. Princeton (1963).

Separate Works:

THE COMICAL REVENGE OR LOVE IN A TUB (1664)

—reprinted 1667, 1669, 1689, 1697.

SHE WOU'D IF SHE COU'D (1668)

—reprinted 1671, 1693, 1710.

THE MAN OF MODE OR SIR FOPLING FLUTTER (1676)

—reprinted 1684, 1693, 1711.

THE LETTERBOOK OF SIR GEORGE ETHEREGE, ed. S. Rosenfeld. Oxford (1928).

Some Biographical and Critical Studies:

SEVENTEENTH CENTURY STUDIES, by E. Gosse (1883).

THE COMEDY OF MANNERS, by J. Palmer (1913).

ESSAYS IN BIOGRAPHY, by B. Dobrée (1925).

Contributions by Dorothy Foster to *NQ*, vols. cliii, 1927 and cliv, 1928, and *RES*, vol. viii, 1932.

ETHEREGE AND THE SEVENTEENTH CENTURY COMEDY OF MANNERS, by D. Underwood. Oxford (1957).

GENERAL WORKS

Bibliography:

A BIBLIOGRAPHY OF ENGLISH POETICAL MISCELLANIES 1521-1750, by A. E. Case (1935).

ENGLISH SONG BOOKS 1651-1702, A BIBLIOGRAPHY, by C. L. Day and E. Boswell. (1940).

Some Biographical and Critical Studies:

ATHENAE OXONIENSES, by Anthony à Wood. 2 vols. (1691-2)
—edited by P. Bliss, 4 vols. 1813-20.

THE LIVES OF THE MOST EMINENT ENGLISH POETS, by S. Johnson. 4 vols. (1781)
—revised edition of 1783 edited by G. B. Hill, 3 vols. Oxford, 1905.

ANECDOTES, OBSERVATIONS AND CHARACTERS OF BOOKS AND MEN COLLECTED FROM THE CONVERSATION OF MR. POPE AND OTHER EMINENT PERSONS OF HIS TIME, by Joseph Spence, ed. S. W. Singer (1820)
—a definitive edition of *Spence's Anecdotes*, edited by J. M. Osborn, will shortly be published by the Oxford University Press.

BRIEF LIVES, by John Aubrey, ed. A. Clark, 2 vols. Oxford (1898)
—edited by A. Powell, 1949.

CRITICAL ESSAYS OF THE SEVENTEENTH CENTURY, ed. J. E. Spingarn. 3 vols. Oxford (1908).

'The Court Poets', by C. Whibley. In *CHEL*, viii (1912).

REVALUATION, by F. R. Leavis (1936).

THE COURT WITS OF THE RESTORATION, by J. H. Wilson. Princeton (1948).

RESTORATION CARNIVAL, by V. de S. Pinto (1954)
—a Folio Society limited edition.

Historical and Social Background:

MÉMOIRES DU CHEVALIER DE GRAMONT, par A. Hamilton. Cologne (1713)
—translated by Peter Quennell, 1930. Edited by C. Engel, Monaco 1958.

THE HISTORY OF MY OWN TIME, by Gilbert Burnet, 2 vols. (1724-34)
—edited by O. Airy, 2 vols. Oxford, 1897-1900.

THE LIFE OF EDWARD EARL OF CLARENDON WRITTEN BY HIMSELF. Oxford (1759)
—2nd edition, 2 vols. Oxford, 1857.

THE DIARY OF JOHN EVELYN, ed. E. S. de Beer, 6 vols. Oxford (1955).

THE DIARY OF SAMUEL PEPYS, ed. H. B. Wheatley. 10 vols. (1893-9).

KING CHARLES II, by A. Bryant (1931).

ENGLAND IN THE REIGN OF CHARLES II, by D. Ogg. 2 vols. Oxford (1956).

POETRY AND POLITICS UNDER THE STUARTS, by C. V. Wedgwood (1960).

POEMS ON AFFAIRS OF STATE vol. I 1660-1678, ed. G. de F. Lord (1963).

WRITERS AND THEIR WORK

General Editor: GEOFFREY BULLOUGH

The first 55 issues in the Series appeared under the General Editorship of T. O. BEACHCROFT

Issues 56-169 appeared under the General Editorship of BONAMY DOBRÉE

General Surveys:

THE DETECTIVE STORY IN BRITAIN: Julian Symons

THE ENGLISH BIBLE: Donald Coggan

ENGLISH HYMNS: A. Pollard

ENGLISH MARITIME WRITING: Hakluyt to Cook: Oliver Warner

THE ENGLISH SHORT STORY I: & II: T. O. Beachcroft

ENGLISH SERMONS: Arthur Pollard

ENGLISH TRAVELLERS IN THE NEAR EAST: Robin Fedden

THREE WOMEN DIARISTS: M. Willy

Sixteenth Century and Earlier:

FRANCIS BACON: J. Max Patrick

CHAUCER: Nevill Coghill

LANGLAND: Nevill Coghill

MALORY: M. C. Bradbrook

MARLOWE: Philip Henderson

MORE: E. E. Reynolds

RALEGH: Agnes Latham

SIDNEY: Kenneth Muir

SKELTON: Peter Green

SPENSER: Rosemary Freeman

WYATT: Sergio Baldi

Seventeenth Century:

SIR THOMAS BROWNE: Peter Green

BUNYAN: Henri Talon

CAVALIER POETS: Robin Skelton

CONGREVE: Bonamy Dobrée

DONNE: F. Kermode

DRYDEN: Bonamy Dobrée

ENGLISH DIARISTS: Evelyn and Pepys: M. Willy

JOHN FORD: Clifford Leech

GEORGE HERBERT: T. S. Eliot

HERRICK: John Press

HOBBES: T. E. Jessop

BEN JONSON: J. B. Bamborough

LOCKE: Maurice Cranston

ANDREW MARVELL: John Press

MILTON: E. M. W. Tillyard

SHAKESPEARE: C. J. Sisson

SHAKESPEARE:

CHRONICLES: Clifford Leech

EARLY COMEDIES: Derek Traversi

FINAL PLAYS: F. Kermode

GREAT TRAGEDIES: Kenneth Muir

HISTORIES: L. C. Knights

LATER COMEDIES: G. K. Hunter

POEMS: F. T. Prince

PROBLEM PLAYS: Peter Ure

ROMAN PLAYS: T. J. B. Spencer

THREE METAPHYSICAL POETS: Margaret Willy

IZAAK WALTON: Margaret Bottrall

WEBSTER: Ian Scott-Kilvert

WYCHERLEY: P. F. Vernon

Eighteenth Century:

BERKELEY: T. E. Jessop

BLAKE: Kathleen Raine

BOSWELL: P. A. W. Collins

BURKE: T. E. Utley

BURNS: David Daiches

WM. COLLINS: Oswald Doughty

COWPER: N. Nicholson

CRABBE: R. L. Brett

DEFOE: J. R. Sutherland

FIELDING: John Butt

GAY: Oliver Warner

GIBBON: C. V. Wedgwood

GOLDSMITH: A. Norman Jeffares

GRAY: R. W. Ketton-Cremer

HUME: Montgomery Belgion

JOHNSON: S. C. Roberts

POPE: Ian Jack

RICHARDSON: R. F. Brissenden

SHERIDAN: W. A. Darlington

CHRISTOPHER SMART: G. Grigson

SMOLLETT: Laurence Brander

STEELE AND ADDISON: A. R. Humphreys

STERNE: D. W. Jefferson

SWIFT: J. Middleton Murry

HORACE WALPOLE: Hugh Honour

Nineteenth Century:

MATTHEW ARNOLD: Kenneth Allott

JANE AUSTEN: S. Townsend Warner

BAGEHOT: N. St. John-Stevas

THE BRONTË SISTERS: P. Bentley

BROWNING: John Bryson

ELIZABETH BARRETT BROWNING: Alethea Hayter

SAMUEL BUTLER: G. D. H. Cole

BYRON: Herbert Read

CARLYLE: David Gascoyne

LEWIS CARROLL: Derek Hudson

CLOUGH: Isobel Armstrong

COLERIDGE: Kathleen Raine

DE QUINCEY: Hugh Sykes Davies

DICKENS: K. J. Fielding
DISRAELI: Paul Bloomfield
GEORGE ELIOT: Lettice Cooper
SUSAN FERRIER & JOHN GALT:
W. M. Parker
FITZGERALD: Joanna Richardson
MRS. GASKELL: Miriam Allott
GISSING: A. C. Ward
THOMAS HARDY: R. A. Scott-James
and C. Day Lewis
HAZLITT: J. B. Priestley
HOOD: Laurence Brander
G. M. HOPKINS: Geoffrey Grigson
T. H. HUXLEY: William Irvine
KEATS: Edmund Blunden
LAMB: Edmund Blunden
LANDOR: G. Rostrevor Hamilton
EDWARD LEAR: Joanna Richardson
MACAULAY: G. R. Potter
MEREDITH: Phyllis Bartlett
JOHN STUART MILL: M. Cranston
WILLIAM MORRIS: P. Henderson
NEWMAN: J. M. Cameron
PATER: Iain Fletcher
PEACOCK: J. I. M. Stewart
ROSSETTI: Oswald Doughty
RUSKIN: Peter Quennell
SIR WALTER SCOTT: Ian Jack
SHELLEY: Stephen Spender
SOUTHEY: Geoffrey Carnall
R. L. STEVENSON: G. B. Stern
SWINBURNE: H. J. C. Grierson
TENNYSON: F. L. Lucas
THACKERAY: Laurence Brander
FRANCIS THOMPSON: P. Butter
TROLLOPE: Hugh Sykes Davies
OSCAR WILDE: James Laver
WORDSWORTH: Helen Darbishire

Twentieth Century:

W. H. AUDEN: Richard Hoggart
HILAIRE BELLOC: Renée Haynes
ARNOLD BENNETT: F. Swinnerton
EDMUND BLUNDEN: Alec M. Hardie
ELIZABETH BOWEN: Jocelyn Brooke
ROBERT BRIDGES: J. Sparrow
ROY CAMPBELL: David Wright
JOYCE CARY: Walter Allen
G. K. CHESTERTON: C. Hollis
WINSTON CHURCHILL: John Connell
R. G. COLLINGWOOD: E.W.F. Tomlin
I. COMPTON-BURNETT:
Pamela Hansford Johnson
JOSEPH CONRAD: Oliver Warner

WALTER DE LA MARE: K. Hopkins
NORMAN DOUGLAS: Ian Greenlees
T. S. ELIOT: M. C. Bradbrook
FIRBANK & BETJEMAN: J. Brooke
FORD MADOX FORD: Kenneth Young
E. M. FORSTER: Rex Warner
CHRISTOPHER FRY: Derek Stanford
JOHN GALSWORTHY: R. H. Mottram
ROBERT GRAVES: M. Seymour-Smith
GRAHAM GREENE: Francis Wyndham
L. P. HARTLEY & ANTHONY POWELL:
P. Bloomfield and B. Bergonzi
A. E. HOUSMAN: Ian Scott-Kilvert
ALDOUS HUXLEY: Jocelyn Brooke
HENRY JAMES: Michael Swan
JAMES JOYCE: J. I. M. Stewart
RUDYARD KIPLING: Bonamy Dobrée
D. H. LAWRENCE: Kenneth Young
C. DAY LEWIS: Clifford Dyment
WYNDHAM LEWIS: E. W. F. Tomlin
KATHERINE MANSFIELD: Ian Gordon
JOHN MASEFIELD: L. A. G. Strong
SOMERSET MAUGHAM: J. Brophy
GEORGE MOORE: A. Norman Jeffares
EDWIN MUIR: J. C. Hall
J. MIDDLETON MURRY: Philip Mairet
GEORGE ORWELL: Tom Hopkinson
POETS OF 1939-45 WAR:
R. N. Currey
POWYS BROTHERS: R. C. Churchill
J. B. PRIESTLEY: Ivor Brown
HERBERT READ: Francis Berry
FOUR REALIST NOVELISTS:
Vincent Brome
BERTRAND RUSSELL: Alan Dorward
BERNARD SHAW: A. C. Ward
EDITH SITWELL: John Lehmann
OSBERT SITWELL: Roger Fulford
C. P. SNOW: William Cooper
STRACHEY: R. A. Scott-James
SYNGE & LADY GREGORY:
E. Coxhead
DYLAN THOMAS: G. S. Fraser
EDWARD THOMAS: Vernon Scannell
G. M. TREVELYAN: J. H. Plumb
WAR POETS: 1914-18: E. Blunden
EVELYN WAUGH: Christopher Hollis
H. G. WELLS: Montgomery Belgion
CHARLES WILLIAMS: J. Heath-Stubbs
VIRGINIA WOOLF: Bernard Blackstone
W. B. YEATS: G. S. Fraser
ANDREW YOUNG & R. S. THOMAS:
L. Clark and R. G. Thomas